Please
Write Soon

Please Write Soon

MICHAEL ROSEN
Illustrated by MICHAEL FOREMAN

■ SCHOLASTIC

Published in the UK by Scholastic, 2022
Euston House, 24 Eversholt Street, London, NW1 1DB
Scholastic Ireland, 89E Lagan Road, Dublin Industrial Estate, Glasnevin, Dublin, D11 HP5F

SCHOLASTIC and associated logos are trademarks and/or
registered trademarks of Scholastic Inc.

Text © Michael Rosen, 2022
Illustrations © Michael Foreman, 2022
Afterword text © Lieutenant General James Bashall CB, CBE, 2022

Image Credits:
Page 68, London, UK. 09th Nov, 2014. cenotaph, Whitehall, Marc Zakian / Alamy Stock Photo
Page 70, Poppy Field, RBL/Joseph Hayes
Page 73, Remembrance Glade, t RBL/Matt Alexander
Page 74, Bethnal Green Underground Station with the Stairway to Heaven Memorial to 173 victims
of the 1943 Bethnal Green Tube disaster, Robert Evans / Alamy Stock Photo

The right of Michael Rosen and Michael Foreman to be identified
as the author and illustrator of this work has been asserted by them
under the Copyright, Designs and Patents Act 1988.

HB ISBN 978 07023 30318 0
PB ISBN 978 0 702 31640 1

A CIP catalogue record for this book
is available from the British Library.

Printed in Malaysia
Paper made from wood grown in sustainable forests and other controlled sources.

1 3 5 7 9 10 8 6 4 2

While the events described and some of the characters in this book may be based on actual historical events and real
people, the characters created by the author are fictional and their stories a work of fiction.

www.scholastic.co.uk

*This book is dedicated to
my father's cousin, Michael Rechnic (1923–2021),
whose real-life experiences during World War II
provided the inspiration for Bernie's story.*

— MR

September 7, 1946

"I hope I will not have to remind you all," Miss Drury said in her precise, clipped way, "that you will listen carefully to each other this morning."

There was a small sigh. Miss Drury glanced up, surprised that someone – anyone – in the class might not be happy with what she wanted them to do. She tilted her head so that her eyes disappeared behind the glare from the windows on her glasses. It was all she needed to do to create complete silence. Late summer sunlight angled its way into the corners of the room and created hotspots on the children's uniforms. As it was the beginning of the new year, some of these were still crisp and new and just that bit too big because the children's parents were trying to avoid having to buy another outfit too soon. "It's all right," their parents had said, "you'll grow into it," when their son or daughter had groaned, worried that their friends would mock sleeves that covered their hands.

Miss Drury had seen it all before.

There were people in her class, especially the girls, who thought that she had been teaching at the school since the times of Henry VIII. Come to that, they thought, she had probably *taught* Henry VIII.

She tilted her head again, this time towards Solomon, a smiley, shambly lad, whom Miss Drury had marked out as someone she had to keep her eye on. *Very bright*, she had noted in her very private "class profile" book that only she ever saw.

Very bright, probably too bright for his own good. Will end up being prime minister or a master criminal. It was one of Miss Drury's jokes to herself. Even so, she had spotted something about Solomon that she wanted to encourage. Apart from anything else, she thought to herself, encouraging the boy would keep him from falling by the wayside. He might well find that he could redirect his "vim" – her favourite word to describe boys' energy – into something constructive.

Solomon – or Solly, as everyone apart from Miss Drury called him – was cheerily unaware of his English teacher's opinions about him. He saw the head tilt in his direction, stopped flicking the cigarette card of Cliff Bastin, his favourite footballer, in his pocket and straightened up.

CLIFF BASTIN

"Solomon," Miss Drury said, smiling for the first time so far, "let us start with you. May I ask you, have you begun the project?"

Solomon stood up. "Yes, Miss Drury, I have begun the project." (Whole sentences was how Miss Drury liked it.)

"And?" she asked, not obeying her own rule about whole sentences.

Solly knew what to do next. He started to read from a piece of paper, on which he had written:

"My project is about my Polish cousin Bernie who was fighting in the war and..."

There was the tiniest of snorts from someone who didn't like Solomon, and whom Solomon didn't like back.

Miss Drury heard it. She stood up. Solomon stopped. Miss Drury had her suspicions as to who it might have been, but she couldn't be sure. The glasses glared. There was a silence even heavier than before.

"And?" Miss Drury prompted Solly once more.

"…and we received letters from him which we have kept. I have brought some of them here."

Miss Drury found herself to be genuinely interested in what Solly was saying. Privately, ever so privately and sadly, the mere mention of letters from a soldier at war had triggered in Miss Drury a pool of sadness that she hardly dared look into. It was an un-secret secret in the school that the reason why Miss Drury was a "miss" was that she had once been madly in love (as the schoolchildren put it) with a man who went off to fight in the First World War and never came back. And the pain of this, according to the secret, was why she had never married. At the Remembrance Day assembly every year, people hardly dared to look at her as she sat, stood, and sat down again, her face and shoulders held firm and unchanging. The poppy she wore seemed redder than anyone else's.

"Solomon," Miss Drury said, turning her mind away from that pool of grief, still full thirty years after it had filled up, "these letters. Are you going to read from them?"

"Yes, I will, Miss Drury," Solly said, "and I will also read from my letters to my cousin."

"Very well," Miss Drury said, "you may begin."

September 1, 1939

Dear Bernie,

Today I lost my marbles.

Do you know what that means? It means I've gone crazy!

But the thing is I <u>did</u> lose my marbles. And I am so sorry. You know what I'm talking about? Those lovely ball bearings you brought over that time you stayed with us. Shiny and heavy. I lost them. You said that your dad gave them to you from the factory where he worked. And do you remember how we named them after our favourite singers and musicians? I said one of them was "Fats" (after Fats Waller) and you said one of them should be "Django" after Django Reinhardt. Do you remember Uncle Morry who's in a dance band? And his gramophone records?

When we go over there for Friday nights he plays Fats Waller and Django Reinhardt and I always think of the ball bearings! Mum's playing Fats Waller tunes on our old piano now. It reminds us all of Dad.

I loved it when you came and we played soccer in Vicky Park. I remember how you showed me that trick where you passed the ball behind your leg. I think I can do it now! When I show my friends I call it "Doing the Bernie"!

Mum took me to see the Arsenal the other day. I was down the front like it was that great time when you came to Highbury with us. Do you remember how Mum seemed to be about the only woman there? And when she started singing, some horrible bloke tried to make her stop it and "go back to the kitchen", but she sang, "You'll never keep me qui-et"! What a squash! That was the season we won the First Division. Good news is that we won - against Chelsea, one nil. Bad news, we're out the Cup. Guess who knocked us out? Chelsea!

Anyway, back with the ball bearings. You see, the thing is I played marbles with them. In the playground at school. Mum said that I shouldn't, but I knew that they would be so good. I knew that they would pulverize the other kids' marbles. Mum put them in her button box so I wouldn't keep seeing them, but actually I love her button box full of buttons of different colours, some covered in cloth, some leather ones. I'm thinking now how me, you and Mum played games with them: lining them up on the kitchen table and flicking them at each other! Well, after Mum went to work (she's still a nurse at the London Hospital), I went to the button box, took out Fats and Django, and went off to play with other kids.

What I didn't expect was that this boy, Max, had a giant glass marble that he calls "Cloudy" and he whammed Fats and Django full on.

I lost them. Both of them. I am so sorry. I hope you don't mind too much. Maybe next time you come over you could bring some more from your dad's factory?

Mind you, some people are saying here that there's going to be another war. Do you think so? Are people saying that in Poland?

Another thing. I seem to remember you were brilliant at whistling. What was that tune you whistled to me? What was it called?

Tell me where you are, and what you're doing.

Lots of love,
Solly

October 15, 1939

Dear Solly,

I write this from the train and will post later when it is possible. Why am I on train? Because Mami and Tatte say that it dangerous now in the west Poland, so I have to go to the east Poland and stay with Tatte's brother and his wife. I know it is hard to understand, but the German army (the Nazis) come in the west and the Russian army (the Soviets) come in the east. Foreigners stand on Poland: one Nazi foot, one Soviet foot. Mami and Tatte say that it will be safer for me on the Russian side of Poland. They say Nazi people hate us Jews, maybe Russians not so much. But I don't know if is true. But what is true, not true? Do you know the differences, Solly?

And if it was not safe for me in the west, is it not safe also for Mami and Tatte? I feel sad now to think about it.

I got on train with one bag that we pack very quick. I lean out of the window and wave to Mami and Tatte. They stand on the platform waving back. I see them in my eye now.

They both in black coats. Again and again they wave till the train go round corner and gone. I think Mami was with tears. Please tell your mum. I know she will want to know how her sister was.

The train is full up. Very full up. Babies are crying and there is no food. Mami pack some bread and chopped herring for me. I remember how you love the chopped herring. Me too. Now I must make it last till we get to the east Poland.

There are some alte kackers on the train. You remember

these Yiddish words I told you? It means "old men", but a bit vulgar too! Some people cry, not just babies. No one knows what is going to happen. People on train saying that Russians will not let us into east Poland and they will make us go back.

I look out window and when a village pass, I imagine I am in village and all is safe. Why is war? There was war to end wars twenty years ago, or so they said, and now another war. Why do these other countries want to have Poland? I ask questions, questions, questions. Sorry if they too hard for you.

Now your country in war too. People very afraid that there will be bombs. Falling from the sky on to houses full of people. That's what they say. Do people say that in London?

In your letter there were many questions. I answer the one about the whistling. I think the one you like is "Bei Mir Bistu Sheyn", but maybe you know that now. It means, "I think you are beautiful". Everyone sing this. I make extra notes when I whistle it, and this you like. I will go stand in the passageway, I will put my head out of window, and whistle it, and think of you.

Hey! And don't get <u>shpilkes</u> about the ball bearings! (You
remember <u>shpilkes</u>? That means don't get worried!) All
will be good.

Love to you and your mum,
Bernie

September 25, 1940

Dear Bernie,

Are you still at your uncle and aunt's place in eastern Poland?

I've been listening to the radio whenever I can, hoping to hear about what's happening where you are. I so hope you are safe. And Mami and Tatte too, back at your home. Have you heard from them? Sometimes I get frightened thinking about these things.

I'm guessing you don't know what's going on here.

I was in bed and I heard this loud hum and then huge crashing sounds. I could feel it. It felt like a giant was shaking the house. I called out for Mum, and she said we had to sit under the table because it was safer there.

In the morning they said Hitler is bombing us.
Whole houses round our way have just disappeared.
People are being killed.

Then they said that the children have got to go away. Mum took me to the station and it was full of kids. It looked like thousands of us. Everyone was saying the names of places, shouting them out, and I was getting muddled and in a panic. I didn't know if I was in the right queue. There were children crying. Mum said I'd be all right, but I could see she was worried too.

I was on a train with loads of other kids whom I didn't know, and I sat wondering and wondering where was I going. I thought of you on your train. Some of the kids here are with their brothers and sisters, and I really wanted you to be here too. I kept saying to myself that wherever we're going, it'll be safer. Then I thought: maybe I'll end up staying in some place where the people will hate me and beat me and I got scared all over again.

Anyway, in the end we got to a station and there were people there to meet us. They were choosing which ones to have! That felt very strange. And, you're not going to believe this: I'm living on a farm! Not with Mum. It's in Herefordshire. Have you ever heard of it? I hadn't!

Mum has to stay in London to nurse the people getting hurt from the bombs. So that's both of us not with our parents, isn't it? I sometimes have bad dreams about the hospital getting bombed while Mum is in there. Do you think that could happen?

The whole world seems dangerous now.

Here, though, I help the farmer and his wife, and I like that. Their children do loads of work on the farm. You should see their hands! So rough! And they know so much stuff about what to do. They've shown me how to collect the eggs from under the chickens in the morning. They're still warm. On a cold morning, I hold them in my hand to warm up my hands. It's lovely!

Sometimes, you have to push the chickens off the eggs to collect them. They look at you like they're bossy old men, but they move if you're firm with them.

The farmer says that soon he's going to show me how to milk a cow. Can you imagine that? They're huge! And if they're cross, they kick. I'm scared, but at the same time I still want to learn how. When the farmer does the milking it sounds like he's peeing in a bucket!

Sometimes things are not so good at school.

The other kids think that I talk funny and keep saying "'appy 'olidays" at me. "Why don't you say 'happy' or 'holidays' like we do?" they say.

There's a boy who doesn't like me. He makes up names about me to make the other kids laugh: "Silly Solly", and much worse. Someone must have told him that my father died and he made up this thing about "Solly lost his daddy", and I got really angry and pushed him, he pushed me back, and next thing we were fighting.

It was just what he wanted, and he was smashing me up. All the other kids were shouting, "Fight! Fight! Fight!"

The teacher came out and we both got the cane. I don't know how to stop that boy from picking on me.

Sometimes it's not so bad. One funny thing the other children taught me:

"Inky pinky ponky,
the farmer bought a donkey.
The donkey died,
the farmer cried,
inky pinky ponky."

What do you think?

I so hope to see you again someday.
Here's a drawing I did of the farm:

I hope you can write to me soon to say what's happening.

Lots of love,
Solly

November 4, 1940

Dear Solly,

I can write very few words. Here is what happen: I get
with my uncle and aunt in eastern Poland, but it become
Russia. I am young and strong, so men come and they say
I must help Russia by going to a Work Camp. I go on
a train again! Now I am far away from Uncle and
Aunt and far, far away from Mami and Tatte.
    Every day I cut trees, chop the trees
into slices, put them on to trucks. It is
big, hard work. My muscles grow.
I am like King Kong.

Some days we stand in cold water up to the knees and my foots get freezing. Some older men find it too hard. They cannot continue. They fall down and don't get up. We have very little food.

They tell us that we work to help Mother Russia.

I get letters from Mami and Tatte. Please tell your mum. They say things are not good in the west. The Nazis hate Jews, they hate Poles, and terrible things happen to everyone. I am worried for them.

I am pleased you are safe on your farm. I hope that Mum is safe too. Such worries with bombs that drop and blow everything up. What a terrible, crazy time for everyone. People just want to live, have family, have good time, be proud of something. And now this. When will the horrible things end?

When we meet up, I am so strong, I pick you up and throw you in air.

Lots of love and to your mother also,
Bernie

April 15, 1941

Dear Bernie,

Since I wrote last time, so much has happened. Mr Churchill said we won the Battle of Britain and our teacher at the school wrote on the board what he said: "Never in the field of human conflict was so much owed by so many to so few", though Mum says that the bombs are still dropping. The teachers tell us about cities other than London where the bombing goes on and so many people have been killed.

Sometimes when I'm going to sleep, I don't know if I'm scared or sad, or both.

Some days here, you wouldn't know the war was going on. The cows munch the grass, the chickens lay eggs, the birds sing, the sheep do daft things. One of them rolled over in the grass and got stuck on his back, and the farmer said we had to help him turn over and get him to stand up. He said something funny to me then. He said, "You were scared he was going to die, weren't you?" I didn't say anything.

Then he said, "That's it with you city kids. You think you're tough, but you're not ready for what happens. We're like animals. We live, we die." Another time, when we were in the upper field, he stared at me hard in the face and said, "I was once in a place where it was 'Kill or be killed'. Think about that, laddie."

It's been a bit of time since I heard from you. I hope you get this letter and I hope you will write soon.

Lots of love,
Solly

December 13, 1941

Dear Bernie,

I don't know whether you've written and the letter has got lost, or maybe my letters haven't reached you and you're fed up with me for not writing, or what.

This summer I heard that the Nazis invaded eastern Poland and then into Russia. The moment I heard that, I thought, that's where Bernie is. It must be terrible that you went to the east because you would be safer there and then you had to go to the Work Camp and now the Nazis are coming. I have no idea what you will do or where you will go. And what's happening to Mami, Tatte and the rest of your family? Mum says she feels bad that she can't help her own sister.

The huge news here is that America has joined the war. Maybe you heard that the Japanese bombed a place called Pearl Harbor and a few days later Hitler declared war on America. Did you hear that? Now, Germany, Japan and Italy are at war with the rest of the whole world!

We have a globe at school and I look at it and imagine bombers flying round it trying to blow the whole world up. In the middle of all this, it's good to think of other things. The farmer's kids told me that they reckoned that there are badgers up in the woods because they've seen their paw prints. They said we could go up there in the evening, hide in a bush and we would see them come out of their holes. So that's what we did. We waited for a night when the moon was out and we went up there at about five o'clock, wrapped in blankets, with sandwiches and drinks, and we waited. Sure enough, after a bit, we heard this shuffling, snuffling noise, and first one badger, then another,

and then two or three more came out. They ran about like they were chasing each other. You could see their eyes catch the moonlight. It was so exciting to see them, and I couldn't help think how amazing it was that there they were, minding their own business, not knowing anything at all about all these things going on in the world. For a moment, it felt like they were cleverer than all of us, just living in their holes and tunnels, coming out to find worms and berries, and going back down. I wanted to be a badger! Then I thought about how Mum has been writing to me about shelters. They're like badgers' tunnels!

Do you know about these? We call them "air-raid shelters" and there are all sorts: some in people's back gardens and yards, Mum says, and in London people go into the Underground and sit on the platforms. You remember them? That time we went on the Underground to London Zoo? That's where they go at night to get away from the bombs. Maybe if I go back to London, I'll go down there too. So that's what I thought about looking at the badgers.

Please, please write, Bernie. I'm getting so worried now.

Lots of love,
Solly

March 11, 1942

Dear Solly,

I'm in army! It was bad in Work Camp. More and more men get sick and die. Some get hurt and their blood go bad. When we meet – and someday we will – I tell you how hard it was. All my bones and muscles in pain and in winter so cold I feel like I'm ice. The Russian guard men hate us and kick us and tell us we are nothing more than worms. Many of us have families in the west where the Nazis rule, but Russia and the Nazis have agreement not to fight.

But then suddenly – ALL CHANGE! They tell us agreement is over – finished. Then, Nazis come to the east, cross Poland, into Russia, and now we all at war with Nazis. Now we are on same side as Russia, same side as the bad guards who beat us! Now we supposed to be big friends! I can't believe what I hear.

Then, man called General Anders is leader of Poles here. We are in his army. We follow him. They teach me how to use gun and shoot. Your farmer say, "Kill or be killed."

That's me now. We go left, right, left, right. We march. We aim guns and fire guns. No one knows where we going. Some say we go to England. Some say we join Red Army and fight Hitler. Some say we go to Persia and Iraq.

I have not heard from Mami or Tatte for long time. Please tell your mum. We hear story that the Nazis make special places in cities for Jews and no one get in or get out.

They are locked in. Some say that the Nazis make camps for Jews and work them till they die. I am scared so much for Mami, Tatte and the family. Mami will not live like this. It's too hard. They don't deserve this. No one deserve this.

I don't know next time I write, dear Solly, and I don't know where I'll be. Send much love to Mum.

Love,
Bernie

October 30, 1942

Dear Bernie,

I'm back with Mum in London!

   I know I got lonely on the farm, but there's things
I miss back there: collecting the eggs, milking the cows,
riding the horse - did I tell you they taught me how
to do that? I fell off once, but it didn't hurt! Well,
not much. And the badgers. I miss the badgers and
their tunnels. Do you know while I was there, one of
the London kids tried to run away? She started to
walk home. They found her miles from where she was
staying and brought her back. Then there was another
kid who went missing, they spent hours looking for
him in the fields and in the woods, and do you know
what happened? Hours later they found him hiding
under his bed!

   We never know when the bombs might drop. Hitler sends
them to cities all over the country, anywhere.
There are places near here that are all smashed up.

Whole streets are down, with great holes in the ground. We're not allowed anywhere near them, but when no one's looking some of us kids go and muck about in there. You never know what you might find: stuff left over. One kid found a tin box with money in it! Another one found a watch. Sometimes we find bottles, stand them up and pelt them with stones like we're fighter planes firing at them.

There's not so much food here. Everything's rationed. That means we are only allowed the amounts of stuff that they say we can have. They've just rationed soap. I'm not that bothered, but I heard Mum crying about it. "We'll be filthy!" she kept saying. "Filthy! I can't stand it!"

Some of the kids at school say that their older brothers and dads are away at the war. Mum listens to the radio and repeats what they say. I don't understand much of it, but I listen out to see if they'll ever talk about your army. "Tell me if they mention Anders' Army," I say. "Cousin Bernie's with Anders' Army!" But these days it's all about General Montgomery in North Africa, who they say is beating some Nazi called Rommel.

I keep wondering which way you went with your army: to Britain, or stayed in Russia, or did you go to Persia? I try to imagine you in a uniform marching with loads of other men, just like I've seen in films.

The other day one of the girls in our class heard that her dad had been killed. It feels like it can happen to anyone anytime. You must know that better than me. Please write to me as soon as you can. If I was you, I would be so scared.

Lots of love,
Solly

February 16, 1943

Dear Solly,

We are in Persia!

I learn how to drive jeep. American jeep! If you here I would say, "Get in jeep, Solly! Hold on, I drive fast!"

They say we will have battle in Iraq. You look at your map in school and go find Persia, Iraq. You see how long way it is from Poland! This war is all over world.

Now story you will not believe, Solly. One of our soldiers is a bear! I see your face laughing. What is it you say — "You pulling the leg"? Here is story: group of soldiers meet Persian boy on the railway station. He has little baby bear who has no mother or father because hunters kill them. They buy baby bear! Next, remember, we have with us many women and children refugees, people fleeing their home countries. One young woman is called Inka. She say she want bear! But she can't keep bear, so bear comes to us soldiers! We call him Wojtek — happy warrior!

He drink our sweet condensed milk from bottles.

He start to eat fruits, honey and sometimes drink beer. You remember how you and me did wrestles? Wojtek does wrestles! When we march, he marches.

Also here it get very, very cold at night. If you lucky, Wojtek keep you warm! He is big, warm blanket!

You tell friends at school. We have bear in our army! This way we win!

We hear news that Hitler lose giant battle at Stalingrad. I think you must hear that news too. I think maybe war end soon.

I don't get letters from Poland. No letters from Mami and Tatte. I worry about this. We hear terrible things happen in Poland. No one is safe. If you hear news on BBC please, please tell. Or ask teachers.

Please, please stop playing in places where bombs fall. Some bombs fall but don't explode. You boys play there, and bomb can explode. Also the houses can fall on you. I tell you, you must stop.

I have told Wojtek, and he says, "Solly, don't play where the bombs fall!" Wojtek is clever bear. He knows everything!

Much love to you and your dear mum.
Bernie

May 3, 1943

Dear Bernie,

You never guess what happened on May 1st?

Arsenal got through to the Football League South War Cup Final!

Next question: where was it held?

Empire Stadium Wembley!

Next question: who went to watch the game?

I bet you got that one: me and Mum. The place was packed. People said that there were 75,000 of us there.

Right, now here's your hardest question: what was the final score? Did Charlton beat us 2-nil? Did we scrape a 2-1 win with a lucky penalty? Or just for fun: do you think we won 7-1?

Are you ready for the answer?

We won 7-1!

Before the game, the players who are soldiers paraded in front of us in their uniforms, and when I saw them

I thought of you. One of our players in uniform is called Denis Compton and he's going to be really good for us. He scored twice. And he's fantastically good at cricket too! Oh sorry, you don't know about cricket, do you?

Now something awful,
I'm afraid. A few weeks
before this great match, in
March, there was a disaster not
far from us: at Bethnal Green
Underground Station. You remember I
told you that people use the stations
as air-raid shelters? Well, the air-raid warning went off
and hundreds of people rushed to Bethnal Green Station.
I've been there with Mum loads of times. The terrible
thing that happened is that people rushed down the steps
into the station, and people who were there say that
someone fell over at the bottom, people fell on top of
her, but more and more people kept on pouring down the
steps and falling on top of the people in front of them.
It's like a nightmare: a great river of people unable to
stop, ending up crushed. It's shocked everyone, people can't
stop talking about it. Sometimes it seems like everyone
knows someone who died in the disaster. It all happened
just round the corner from where Mum used to live and
where she went to school, when she was a girl.

What I didn't say before about going to Wembley was that we went by train, and when we walked down the steps and there were hundreds of people pushing and shoving, I thought of the Bethnal Green disaster and I have to say I was scared. I hung on to Mum for dear life. She said, "Come on, Solly, don't be a shlemiel!" Do you remember she always calls me that?

I often think about you, and when we don't hear from you, we get worried. Not much news gets to us about your Polish Army. There was one rumour that said that you might be going to Italy, but Uncle Morrie said that was bupkis. Do you say that word? It means rubbish or nonsense.

I really look forward to hearing from you. Write as soon as you can.

I really hope your mum and dad are all right.

Mum sends her love.

Lots of love from me too,
Solly

May 20, 1944

Dear Solly,

We are in Italy. We fight with British Army against Nazis in Italy. And many more: many Americans, French, Canadians, Indians, New Zealanders, Moroccans.

Do you know what is monastery? Monastery is big building where the monks live. There is mountain here called Monte Cassino. On top of mountain, there is monastery. Big, big monastery, with many walls. Around the monastery or in it, here it is that the German army put men, guns, to stop us going through Italy to Germany. It is very good idea by them to sit on top of the mountain, because they look down on all of us and shoot at us.

The other armies tried three times to get to the top, to win the battle, but they could not. And many, many men die.

Then generals meet up for talks and ask our General Anders to try for the fourth go at the monastery. General Anders say yes and we try to climb mountain. It was most shocking thing. Guns and shells and grenades. Maybe you see film which show you how it is. The noise make your ears go deaf. And you see things make you not want to see. And in the middle, you will not believe, but do you know: Wojtek help us! Men say that they see Wojtek carry our heavy boxes, put them on lorry so we can load our guns.

What happen here at Monte Cassino is biggest danger ever I have seen. And I am in the middle, like Wojtek. It is terrible. I see friends I am with since we were in Russia being killed. I feel very, very sad about that.

After, we hear singers sing a song. In English it has the name: "The Red Poppies on Monte Cassino". The men who make the song are with us - one called Konarski, who write the words, and the other called Schütz, who make the tune.

When we hear the song for first time, many soldiers cry. We
see the poppies on the mountain, beautiful red flowers,
and the poppies tell us of the men
who died on the mountain.

I'm telling you truth, I do not know how I am alive.

And the war is not over. There are many, many miles to get to Berlin. People say the Russians will get there before we do. I don't know what that means for me. I hear nothing from Mami and Tatte. Everyone hears bad things have happened to the Polish cities, Polish people and Polish Jewish people.

Much love to you and to your dear mother also,

Bernie

November 27, 1944

Dear Bernie,

We haven't heard from you for a while. We've read that after Monte Cassino your army has been in some other battles in Italy. We are worried about that because we have not heard. We so hope you are all right.

When Mum read the last line of your last letter she sat me down to talk to me very seriously.

She says that for more than a year she (or people she talks to) have been going to meetings, listening to the radio, and reading articles in the papers at our library, and they think that the Nazis have done terrible things in Poland. They say that the Nazis have made what Mum calls "death camps" where they send all the people they hate: Jews, Poles, Gypsies, Communists and more. Mum says that she didn't want to tell me before because she thought I was too young to know about such things, and she didn't want me to write to you to tell you about it while you were in the middle of battles.

She is as worried as you about what might have happened to Mami and Tatte. The news she's read and heard makes her think that there are hardly any Jewish people left in Poland. I don't know. Can this be possible?

This is a horrible letter to write, Bernie. I'm not supposed to tell you all those things, but I wouldn't like it if you kept stuff like that from me. So I'm telling you. Sometimes it seems like things are getting better. I must say also that the Nazis have other weapons, called rockets. They are flying bombs: bombs that come to London and elsewhere without pilots flying planes and dropping them.

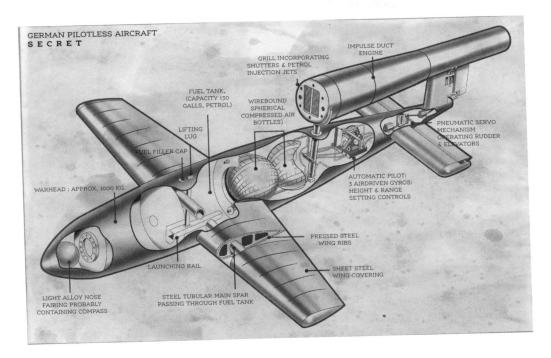

GRILL INCORPORATING
SHUTTERS & PETROL
INJECTION JETS

IMPULSE DUCT
ENGINE

FUEL TANK.
(CAPACITY 130
GALLS, PETROL)

WIREBOUND
SPHERICAL
COMPRESSED AIR
BOTTLES)

LIFTING
LUG

PNEUMATIC SERVO
MECHANISM
OPERATING RUDDER
& ELEVATORS

FUEL FILLER CAP

AUTOMATIC PILOT:
3 AIRDRIVEN GYROS:
HEIGHT & RANGE
SETTING CONTROLS

WARHEAD : APPROX, 1000 KG.

PRESSED STEEL
WING RIBS

LAUNCHING RAIL

SHEET STEEL
WING COVERING

LIGHT ALLOY NOSE
FAIRING PROBABLY
CONTAINING COMPASS

STEEL TUBULAR MAIN SPAR
PASSING THROUGH FUEL TANK

The first ones people called "doodlebugs", and the ones coming now are called "V2s". The doodlebugs made a noise in the sky like a motorbike, but the V2s are silent till they explode. The other night, one of them hit a Woolworths shop in south London and many, many people were hurt, or killed.

It can't be long now, though, that the armies from the west or the east will get to Berlin and stop the war.

I wonder if I'll ever go back to the farm in Herefordshire. If I want to think of peaceful things, I think of the fields and woods and the badgers there.

Lots of love,
hoping to hear from you so much,
Solly

September 20, 1945

Dear Solly,

Thank you for letter from end of last year. This is first letter
from me when there is no war!

  Now it is sad to write that we know that your mother
was right. The soldiers find death camps and now whole world
know what the Nazis did. I hear no news of Mami and Tatte.

I write letters. I ask people who could know, but I hear nothing. I am very sad in my heart that there is no one. I cannot go back where there is nothing. Now Stalin's Russian troops are in Poland too, so I don't want to go back. I feel very upset and empty, but I will never give up. If you never hear from me because bad things happen again, you must know that I never, never give up.

General Anders say that he talk to the British and he will be sure we come to Britain. When I think this, it make me much, much happier. I think of coming to your house and we go to Arsenal. Or even you take me to the farm and we milk cows and look at badger!

Ha ha, now I dream. Dream is good, but after dream there is pain that it is not real.

I think of you and your mum very often. I remember your mum say, "People have to have the hope. If we don't have the hope, we have nothing."

Much love,
Bernie

September 1946

Solly stopped reading.

Miss Drury and the class could see that Solly had read the last letter. There were no letters left in his hand. The class looked at each other. What happened next? What happened to Bernie? Is he alive or was he…? Solly's and Bernie's letters had filled everyone with thoughts, hopes, sadnesses, terrors and many questions.

Miss Drury sensed the mood.

"Well, Solomon, that was extremely interesting. And very, very moving. Before I ask you anything, I think you all have questions to ask, don't you, class?" She looked over the top of her glasses and round the room.

At first, no one quite dared to ask Solly anything. Everyone's mind was full of the scenes he had talked about: trains, badgers, the child who ran away, the steps at Bethnal Green station ... and the logging camp in Russia, the battle at the monastery...

And there were questions that people hardly dared to ask in case they heard the answers. Could they ask Solly if Bernie was alive? What if he hadn't made it, and Solly got upset? And Mami and Tatte? Could they ask about them?

Someone put their hand up.

"Yes?" said Miss Drury.

"I liked what you said about the badgers," he said.

"Thank you," Miss Drury said.

"Do you know where the camp was in Russia?" someone else asked.

"No," said Solly.

Everyone knew that no one had asked the big questions. No one wanted to be the first to ask. Instead, there were other questions about the child who ran away, how Bernie got from Poland to Persia, could Solly show the class how to milk a cow – that made everyone laugh – and this was a moment when everyone could relax. Solly said he could. That was quite funny too, people thought.

There was a pause.

"Any more questions?" Miss Drury asked.

No, there weren't. The class were willing Miss Drury to say what they didn't feel they could ask.

"Solomon," said Miss Drury in a quiet, considerate way, "can I ask you please, what happened..." she hesitated, "...next?"

"Yes," Solly said in his very direct way.

He looked round the room.

"The Polish soldiers and all the Polish refugees who had survived got on boats and came to England. They were put in camps. Most of them are still in the camps. They are old army camps out in the country. They're all living in huts. They are safe, but most of them want to go to Poland – but they won't go back so long as the Russians are running the place. In the meantime they have to stay there. Well, most of them."

Solly could feel the next wave of questions welling up. Miss Drury liked the way that Solly was handling it all by himself, pleased that she had got it right about him.

"One day we were at home. Mum was reading a book. I was in the yard pumping up the tyres on my bike and I heard a whistle. Someone was whistling 'Bei Mir Bistu Sheyn'... The knocker went on our front door. I stopped working on my bike, and I heard a shout, or a scream, and footsteps running towards the front door. I dropped my bicycle pump and ran there too.

"You know what I'm going to say, don't you? It was Bernie! He was so big and strong! He was so big! Last time I saw him he was about fifteen and now he was a man. We all just ran into each other's arms and we cried and cried. What could we say…? What could we say…?"

Saying "what could we say?" took Solly straight back to that moment at the door, when he felt the hugs from Bernie and Mum, and it was as if all the waiting, the worry, the tragedy, the terror all melted into tears.

Solly wiped his face. He put his hand into his pocket and pulled out something that the class couldn't quite see.

"Bernie said, 'I bring you these.' He opened his hand, and there were two ball bearings! Bernie had brought them from home, carried them all through the time with his uncle and aunt, through  the time he was in the Russian camp, through to Persia, through the Battle of Monte Cassino, through the camp in England, right up to our front door."

Solly walked round the class showing everybody. As he walked past one classmate, she asked, "Has he heard from his mum and dad?"

Solly shook his head. He remembered Mum asking Bernie that very same question. Solly shook his head again. Gone, he thought, disappeared, taken away. He remembered Mum's face, the wave of sadness that she would never see her sister and her sister's husband ever again.

In the middle of that feeling came one more question.

"What about Wojtek?"

"Yes," the other children asked, "what about the bear?"

Solly stopped in his tracks. He looked at the class. They really did want to know what happened to Wojtek.

"He's gone to Scotland," Solly said. "A farm in Scotland."

Now everyone wanted to go to the farm in Scotland. Everyone could have a moment to think of things that weren't so sad, weren't so terrible.

Miss Drury took her glasses off.

Took out her hankie. She wiped her eyes.

Put the glasses back on. She didn't say anything.

There really was nothing more to say.

The bell rang. She stood up.

She let the class out. And she

sat down on her own

in the classroom.

Afterword

By Lieutenant General James Bashall CB, CBE

Bernie's story was inspired by the remarkable real-life experiences of a man named Michael Rechnic. And, like Bernie, Michael survived the war and came to live in the United Kingdom. But many of his fellow soldiers did not; about 75,000 soldiers from both sides died in the Battle of Monte Cassino alone, and that was just one of many battles over the course of World War II.

Every November the Royal British Legion leads the country in Remembrance. We think of those whose service and sacrifice created the freedoms we enjoy today. As a nation we mourn the loss of young men and women who died in the service of their country. We remember not only those who fell but those who serve, as well as veterans and their families. However, Remembrance is not just about those who die in war. It is about all people who help and protect others in emergencies, putting service before themselves.

Remembrance unites people of all faiths, cultures and backgrounds but it is also deeply personal. It could mean wearing a poppy in November, before Remembrance Sunday. It could mean joining with others in your community on a commemorative anniversary. Or it could mean taking a moment on your own to pause and reflect. Everyone is free to remember in their own way, or to choose not to remember at all. Remembrance is a time when we give thanks for the people who help and protect others now, and who have done so in the past. We remember those who have been hurt or killed as a result.

November 11th is known as Armistice Day in the United Kingdom. In Ghana, Antigua, and Barbuda it is Remembrance Day. Poland celebrates National Independence Day on November 11th. Whilst also observing Remembrance Day on November 11th, the official day of Remembrance in Australia and New Zealand is the 25th of April. This is known as Anzac Day and recalls the day when forces from those countries first set foot on Gallipoli in 1915.

Why is it important to remember those who died in war? There are many reasons, but the main one is that they gave their lives in the service of their country so that the generations who came after would be able to live in freedom and democracy. Their service and sacrifice have a direct bearing on all our lives, young and old. We also remember the men and women who helped on the home front. The Second World War saw many acts of bravery all over the country by firemen, nurses, police and members of the public who volunteered to help victims of air raids.

Today we remember those who have shown great courage and helped us in more recent times. In 2020 the pandemic created a major emergency for the NHS. Doctors, nurses, ambulance drivers and other key workers put their lives on the line as they tried to help people suffering from Covid-19. The author of this book, Michael Rosen, has written about his own experiences with the virus, and of his gratitude to the hospital care workers who saved his life. Many thousands died in the course of their service. As a nation we remember those who died as well as those who survived. We are grateful to the teachers who kept the schools running for children of the key workers and to the delivery drivers who kept vital supplies to shops.

We mark Remembrance with symbols. The most familiar of all is the red poppy which is worn in the lead-up to 11 November. The poppy became a symbol of Remembrance and hope for a peaceful future in 1921, and it has remained the symbol most closely associated with Remembrance in Britain and many other countries. The French have the cornflower as their symbol. In India and Pakistan, the marigold is the flower of Remembrance. In Italy it is the lily.

There are many other symbols of Remembrance that have evolved more recently. The NHS rainbow appeared in the early months of the pandemic, and today the rainbow is recognized as a symbol of courage and sacrifice of medical professionals all over the country.

We not only have symbols but also acts that we share when we remember people. During the summer of 2020, every Thursday evening people stood at their front doors and clapped for the NHS. That was an act of solidarity to thank those who were helping us to live through the pandemic. When we mark Remembrance in November, we take time to reflect on the human cost of conflict.

The first Remembrance Service was held on 11 November 1921. The simple service has not changed much over the last 100 years. Four lines from a poem were read out. In the Royal British Legion we call it 'The Exhortation'. You might know it better as part of a poem called "For The Fallen".

> *They shall grow not old, as we that we that are left grow old:*
> *Age shall not weary them, nor the years condemn.*
> *At the going down of the sun and in the morning*
> *We will remember them.*

This was a promise made by the poet Laurence Binyon in 1914 after the Battle of the Marne. "We will remember them" is repeated by those gathered at the service. After the poem, Last Post is sounded, usually by a bugler, followed by the Two Minute Silence. This is the moment when the whole country falls silent and reflects on loss. Sometimes two lines, known as the Kohima Epitaph, follow at the end of the service:

> *When you go home, tell them of us and say,*
> *For your tomorrow, we gave our today.*

The poet John Maxwell Edmonds wrote these lines to commemorate the men who died in the Battle of Kohima in India in April 1944. Many of those were volunteers from the Indian subcontinent.

In this book you have read the story of cousins Bernie and Solly who wrote to each other during the Second World War. Bernie's parents were Jews who lived in Nazi-occupied Poland. They were kept in ghettos and then sent to concentration camps, where they died.

We know that because Bernie told Solly about it in his letters. Today the names of the six million Jews like Mami and Tatte are commemorated in a book of Remembrance in Israel. There are monuments to those who died in the Holocaust all over the world.

Solly tells Bernie the story of the tragedy at Bethnal Green Underground Station in 1943. After an air-raid warning there was a crush on the stairs as people tried to get to safety in the underground station. That night 173 people died, including 62 children. It was one of the worst civilian disasters of the Second World War. The Stairway to Heaven Memorial to the dead was unveiled in December 2017, long after the accident. It records the names of all the victims. The memorial is important because it reminds us that civilians died in the Second World War as well as soldiers, sailors and airmen. It also reminds us that children died too, not just adults.

During the coronavirus pandemic, schools were closed at times to all but the children of essential key workers. In a similar way thousands of schools across the UK closed in the autumn of 1939, affecting almost all children, some 3 million of whom became evacuees. There is a memorial in Staffordshire to the evacuee children who left the big towns and cities during the Second World War. You might have learned about the evacuation at school. Imagine how hard it must have been to be separated from your family for months or years. Some children never saw their parents again, because their parents were killed in air raids or died fighting. All these stories need to be remembered. They are part of our family stories, but they are also part of our national stories.

Memorials and monuments are another important sign of Remembrance. The most famous of all in the United Kingdom is the Cenotaph in Whitehall, London. It was unveiled in 1920 and is the centre of the annual act of Remembrance every November. There are many other memorials all over the world. You probably know one in your own area.

At the National Memorial Arboretum in Staffordshire there are memorials to hundreds of different organizations. The largest of all is the Armed Forces Memorial which records the names of those who have died in active service since 1945. The war widows are represented, as are the police, fire service and the air ambulance service. There are memorials to men and women from all over the Commonwealth who volunteered to fight in the British Armed Forces during the Second World War. The Sikh Memorial is just one

you might see at the NMA. The most recent memorial is the Remembrance Glade, where people can sit or stand quietly and think about what Remembrance means to them. It is at the NMA that a memorial to victims of the Covid-19 pandemic will be erected. The names of those who died will be recorded in just the same way and with the same care as those who died in wars. We remember that for every person who died of Covid-19 there is a family whose loss is every bit as painful as those who lost members in war. Remembrance has changed over the years and will continue to develop, but at its core are the people who have passed away.

In 2021 the Royal British Legion celebrated its centenary. On Saturday 15 May 2021, on a damp, grey morning, I stood at the Cenotaph in Whitehall in London with five other people. As Big Ben struck nine o'clock I recited the four lines from "For the Fallen". After that a bugler from the Band of the Welsh Guards sounded Last Post, which was followed by the Two Minute Silence. Then there was the wreath laying ceremony. First came a wreath on behalf of the Royal British Legion. Then five more wreaths: from the Army, the Navy, the Royal Air Force, the Merchant Marine and military widows.

Standing in front of the Cenotaph in silence on that rainy morning, I thought about what Remembrance means to individuals and how the Royal British Legion has helped to promote the act of remembrance over the last 100 years. It is something we will continue to do because the need to remember, to reflect and to celebrate life will never leave us.

Solly and Bernie hugged each other in delight and grief on the doorstep after the war – delight because they were reunited, grief because of what they had lost. A mother and father to Bernie, a sister to Solly's mother, an aunt and uncle to Solly. Together they could grieve and together they would be able to remember. It may have taken years for Bernie to find out where and when his parents died, but that is the great consolation of Remembrance. Even 74 years after the Bethnal Green Tube Station tragedy there was enough care and interest to create a memorial.

During the pandemic we relied on so many people who gave their time, and sometimes their lives, to keep us safe. In addition to the key workers, doctors and nurses, the Armed Forces became involved, as they often do whenever there is a major emergency. They supported the NHS when the Nightingale hospitals were operating, and they helped with the roll-out of the vaccination programme.

The Royal British Legion keeps alive the flame of Remembrance in Britain, but we need your hands to pass it on. You are the custodians of the future of Remembrance. We want to reach out into all communities in this country and to share the importance of recognizing and reflecting on sacrifice and service. As the years go by, it falls to each generation to make Remembrance meaningful, as it will fall to you. That way, we keep the promise in Binyon's poem: "We will remember them."